YOUR INTUITION CALLING

Tune into your inner voice

FRANK KNOLL

DISCLAIMER

Table Of Contents

INTRODUCTION

This book will introduce you to basics about intuition and show you how to use it properly. You will also learn more about the meditation, power of prayer, and all aspects of your mind.

You may be quick to ask what intuition is and you are not alone.

We are all born with a set of powerful abilities and one of them is intuition. As the world changed, we have lost track of this natural ability. But throughout history, we find that intuition has helped us carve our paths.

There is no question that intuition is a God-given ability that we must harness together with meditation and prayer. We should not waste our time in disregarding this powerful ability given to us.

This useful guide is meant for all those who believe in intuition and its immense powers. It should help find that inner voice and reveal to you the right perspective you should observe things from.

This may also be a useful tool for those who are simply beginning their journey into the world of intuition. In every chapter of this book, you will find great stories of people who have saved lives simply by listening to their intuition. If you aren't a believer of how magnificent our intuition is, then the stories that are contained in this book may help you to see how powerful it is.

We are aware that due to the way we live in this era, many have already lost their touch to their natural capabilities. Many people struggle to use intuition on the daily.

There is also a lot to take away from the stories of real people and the information in this book, so make sure to read it to its fullest.

After reading it, you will become richer and more complex as a personality and you will have a powerful tool to use every day - your intuition.

If you are concerned with the state of your intuition, read this wonderful book and see what awaits you!

CHAPTER 1

WHAT IS INTUITION?

The famous and well-regarded spiritual writer, Fr. Richard Rohr, once said, "We often know things imaginably, aesthetically, or harmoniously before we know then rationally or conceptually."

This encompasses what intuition truly is and how we may be able to use it to our success.

This sums up what intuition truly is. It might not be very evident to us, but our minds are very powerful when it comes to noticing minute details in our surroundings. And although it might not be evident, we can already connect a whole host of things without an obvious reason.

1. Talking of what it is and how it relates to thoughts and spiritual health

Before we can start harnessing our intuition, we must first understand what intuition is, only then can we use it to better ourselves.

A common misconception in most circles is that intuition is the same as instinct. They are basically the same but there are a few differences that we need to take note.

Wanting to buy chocolate flavored ice cream every time you go to the ice cream store is different from having an immediate feeling of having to buy strawberry flavored ice cream that day.

To put it simply, instinct is a natural inclination towards a behavior. Instinct is what tells us what brand of car to buy, what flavor of juice drink to get, what restaurant we'd like to dine in. Instinct naturally comes as a product of who we are.

Intuition, on the other hand, is something that comes as we do something, a gut feeling that we get while we are in the moment of things. It is a thought that appears in our minds that tells us to do something different or additional without being fully aware if there are any deep-rooted reasons for its appearance. Some may even call intuition as an inner voice that guides us towards the right decisions.

Intuition is what tells us to use a different route to avoid traffic while we are driving in our car and taking the usual route we use. Intuition is what compels us to buy extra groceries during stormy weather.

There are many ways to define intuition, but in general, it's the ability to know something immediately, without activating analytic reasoning.

We can also call it a connection between two different parts of our mind - conscious and unconscious, or a bridge between reason and instinct.

Animals have instincts, we humans have intuition, but basically, it's the same.

We can also say that intuition is something that lives inside of us, it's deeply rooted, and that's why it has such a strong impact on the way we think, feel, react, etc.

2. Maybe you're already using Intuition or listening to inner voice but need to tune in

A patient in a local hospital had recently finished a minor surgery and was scheduled to be discharged the following day. The nurse tasked to assist the patient throughout his entire stay in the hospital had a sort of bad feeling since her shift began and so checked on the patient multiple times, but the patient reported to be doing fine.

Regardless, the attending nurse still felt something was off and continued to check in with the patient. The patient attempted to walk; he would've walked unsupervised if it weren't for the nurse. The patient after standing up immediately passed out due to life-threatening heart rhythm.

If the nurse hadn't listened to her intuition and simply followed through with what the patient reported and what the records stated, the patient could have been in a much direr situation.

We might not know it, but a lot of lives have been saved either directly or indirectly by people listening to their intuition.

In our culture, intuition is second to rational thinking. Our much advancement in the field of technology and medicine has made us into a society of reason wherein, if something has no obvious rationale to it, we do not entertain it the slightest bit. We were thought in school to think critically about everything that we do – from the food we eat up to the clothes we wear to that very important meeting.

Rational thinking is important of course, but having a culture built around it doesn't lend itself well to intuition.

Intuition is supposed to bridge the gap, to reach into the places where rational thinking could be time-consuming or simply impractical.

All of us were born with intuition and because it is suppressed by the culture that we have created, we must now learn how to harness the immense capabilities that it processes.

Here you can describe how all of us have that inner voice, the feeling that something is about to happen (and it really happens).

People who know themselves better will refer to that inner voice as intuition and will use it frequently and intentionally, to say so. What I mean is that they are AWARE that intuition exists, and they will rely on it.

One of the many examples of the people who use intuition daily is our diligent and hardworking servicemen – from our local sheriff to our boys fighting overseas. Intuition is what helps them decide in split seconds where lives are at stake. They have depended and harnessed the immense capabilities of natural intuition.

But wait, you might be thinking that our servicemen have been trained to use intuition months on end and you might not be up to the task?

As we've mentioned, intuition is natural, everyone has it. We use intuition a lot, we might not notice it, but we do, although in limited form.

The other group of people either refuses to accept that something like that exists at all (as they only rely on their mind and reasonable thinking) or perhaps are not sure how to call it, have doubts whether they should rely on it.

Our society relies mostly on rational thinking, so it is not uncommon to find people who disregard intuition as something made up. People will tag intuition as worthless hearsays, but think about it, you will surely find an instance in your life when intuition saved you. It could have gotten you that big business deal, helped you get through the traffic, or saved you from losing a limb.

That's why it's of vital importance to practice that.

CHAPTER 2

RELAXING THE MIND

When Chloe was 13, she and her sister went to a local pet shop. While inside the establishment, a man entered, and Chloe felt the ambiance change. She felt something terrible as if her gut is telling her to run. She didn't think twice and immediately took her sister and went outside of the pet shop. They went to their mother as they were already finished with the groceries and Chloe took a moment to look back into the store. The place was crowded with uniformed officers and numerous helicopters flew above.

According to her mother, the man who Chloe noticed had attempted to rob the place and had shot the cashier. When Chloe found this out, she realized that her hunch had just saved her life and her sister's. Ever since that day, she had never questioned her intuition.

1. The importance of staying focused on one thing at a time

The current trend of the world is that of a fast-paced living wherein you lose if you aren't ahead on things. Because of this, we are forced to work on a lot of things simultaneously.

Multitasking is what we call this new lifestyle. We see this in a lot of people – from the mother who does two regular jobs while at the same time caring for her child and maintaining a business. Or the recent college graduate who attempts to do a multitude of things in order to climb the corporate ladder. In fact, you could be doing a lot of multitasking yourself; you might even believe that you are an "expert" when it comes to it.

The multitasking culture is upon us, mix it with our hard-working, no-nonsense style and you got yourself a recipe for disaster.

Even though it's widely promoted that people should develop the ability to multitask, they should practice doing the opposite - occupy them with one thing at a time.

Why would multitasking be detrimental to us?

While it might burst some bubbles, countless studies on the fields of Psychology and Neuroscience have shown that multitasking is a myth. It has been shown that rather than increase our productivity, doing multiple things at once does the opposite.

Multitasking splits our focus so many ways that we perform sluggishly on the tasks at hand which uses up valuable time.

Now, what does multitasking have to do with our current state, how does it affect our ability to use our intuition? For one thing, we use less of our intuition the less focus we give it. With our focus split up into so many different things, we drown out our intuition.

For intuition to work, we must give it our unwavering focus and determination.

Intuition is not only important because it aids us in life-threatening situations, but it can also aid us in making important life decisions. The life decisions we make will remain with us throughout our life, that's why we must make sure that our intuition is in top shape.

What happens when our intuition goes out of service?

Ayesha was 25 at the time her intuition went haywire on her. She had a very successful story, a nice apartment, a good-paying job, good health, and able to save up money for the rainy days. It came suddenly to her one day; her intuition was telling her to quit her good paying job and to pursue a low paying job in her local town.

But once she begins to entertain the thought, her intuition would tell her to keep the job, regardless Ayesha was confused.

For the first time, she could not trust her intuition – the same intuition that helped her choose the right decisions. This is the same intuition that gave her such success at 25 years of age.

If you focus your mind and body on a single thing, you will be fully devoted to it and be able to understand it deeply and completely, otherwise, the alleged devotion will be just that- alleged, non-existent.

It's also a skill that we can practice - those common sorts of advice like, turn off the phone, computer and so on, and read the book without checking FB, Twitter, Instagram all the time, and then move on to something more complex.

2. Why there is more noise in today's world pulling us than ever before

Like I mentioned, modern times bring too many distractions (mobile gadgets and social networks), and if we want to learn how to focus on one thing, we should eliminate those obstacles.

With all the distractions that are bombarding us throughout the day, we must attempt to eliminate them. But first, we must accept in ourselves that as humans, we are drawn to distractions.

It is innate to us to follow the latest gadget trends, social media posts, and fads. We must acknowledge that it is a part of us to partake in such activities. Once we accept in ourselves that we are attracted to distractions, we'll have our jobs cut a little shorter.

It won't be an easy process, which is why it will have to be performed gradually.

Here is a couple of Exercises that we could do to jumpstart our inner wellbeing and to improve our intuition:

I.   Start Small

Your intuition might be rusty because of prolonged negligence and so having it started is going to be a huge leap. In any major lifestyle change that we do, we must always start small. You might ask why would we start small, after all, it would be much better if we can have it done in no time? Starting out small helps ourselves acclimate to the new rules of the game; it makes the transition easy enough so that we are not dissuaded in continuing. Starting small has the advantage of having the statistics on our side. Studies show that gradual changes are more successful than large ones.

II.   Make Use of a Journal

If you have ever kept a personal journal, then you know how this would help. Keeping a journal as you gradually improve your intuition helps your coconscious mind to be more open. You can write anything down. Write down your feelings and your thoughts, even the jumble of words and phrases that don't make sense to you

III.   Silence the Critic Within

As mentioned in our previous chapter, our culture gives more emphasis to rationale rather than intuition. Because of this, we drive away from our inner voice by rationalizing them. Allow your inner voice this time; do not criticize your inner voice. Allow it to flourish without the threat of ridicule or fear. When done, you'll find your inner voice being more and more capable as time goes by.

IV.   Find Time to be Alone

Find a quiet place where you can be alone. Being alone in a quiet place helps your emotions to flow without any sort of restriction – a safe space for it to flourish. When your emotions are given the ability to flourish, discovering and retaining the fundamental parts of our intuition occurs. To further enhance this, you may also want to create an attachment to a color, object or anything that will allow you to stir feelings from within.

1. Then to receive/tune into the voice from within

Once we do that "spring-cleaning" and liberate ourselves from those strings, our inner being, and inner voice will be able to breathe and live freely.

This represents a solid foundation for learning how to listen to and rely on intuition, and as we perfect those skills step by step, we will get a sort of inner loyal companion which will guide us through life.

2. Meditation types in the day for focus and relaxation

Meditation is excellent because it helps relieve stress, not only from our mind but the entire body, and we should all practice it every day. We can even refer to it as a necessary activity in this fast-paced life, as a mandatory activity to help us slow down a bit and find some time for ourselves.

There are two basic techniques namely concentrative and non-concentrative. Meditation can be practiced using several different methods; basic, focused, activity-oriented, mindful and spiritual.

Meditation Categories

1. Concentrative

Concentrative meditation simply means that you concentrate on an object outside of yourself. The object you could focus on could be a candle, the sound of instrumentation; it may also be a certain mantra.

2. Non-Concentrative

Non-concentrative meditation differs in that it is broader than concentrative meditation. With this meditation technique, one can make use of anything like ambient sounds, a certain idea, etc.

While there are two techniques considered in meditation, there could be places where overlap occurs and the distinction with both is vague.

Meditation Techniques

Meditation has a lot of ways to perform; the list could become very exhaustive. The following are some of the most regarded techniques in meditation. Think of the following as points to begin your journey into meditation. Also, note that meditation is a valuable tool in harnessing the capabilities of your intuition.

1. Basic Meditation

This is the simplest and widely adopted form of meditation. When you see people meditate on TV, this is what you are seeing. Basic meditation is done by sitting in a comfortable position and having your mind think of nothing in order to attain quiet. While this is the simplest form of meditation, it could be difficult if you are not already a practitioner of it.

To have an easy start, you may want to see yourself as a detached observer. You engage in the inner voice in your mind and you simply let go of any thoughts that you conjure.

2. Focused Meditation

Focused meditation, as the name implies, is the attempt to focus on something with purpose while not entertaining any thoughts that might materialize. For this kind of meditation, you can focus on something auditory (ambient noise), visual (the flame of a candle), or even a simple concept like kindness, or a longing for something.

To help you begin, people who practice Focus Meditation find it easier to focus on nothing. Yes, nothing! But the idea remains, remaining at the present while letting the comments from your conscious mind flow without a second thought. While doing so, you allow yourself to move into the altered state of consciousness.

3. Activity-Oriented Meditation

Activity oriented meditation is a technique in meditation wherein meditation is combined with the activities that you are already into. It could also be a mix of meditation and any new activities that would allow you to focus on the present.

This meditation where you perform repetitive actions, you can get into it without an afterthought. Under this technique, common activities like painting, practicing yoga, and similar activities can be highly effective. Although these may not sound like meditation, it would be effective, as long as it quiets the mind and allows your mind to shift into the altered state of consciousness.

4. Spiritual Meditation

Meditation is not a practice isolated towards a single religion, but it cannot be discounted that it can be a form of spiritual practice. A great lot of people see meditation as a form of prayer. Once the mind has been placed in a quiet state, people who practice this seek inner wisdom and guidance.

People sense God as speaking to them while in this meditation. To perform this, one can focus on a single question until an answer arrives or until the mind is cleared and one is prepared for the day.

5. Mindfulness Meditation

Mindfulness meditation could have similarities to activity-oriented meditation that was previously discussed. One thing that might be apparent with both is that it might not look like meditation.

This form of meditation has a focus on the present rather than the past or the future. Also, just like activity-oriented meditation, this might be easier said than done. One thing that might help is to attempt to focus on the sensations felt throughout your body. Take note that you do not analyze the sensations but simply feel them as they are.

Being in the now, quiet mind, and achieving an altered state of consciousness are key objectives of every type of meditation. They represent the needed condition we have to find ourselves in to be able to meditate the right way.

Basics of Meditation

Meditation can be fulfilled in many ways, and they all follow three fundamentals:

1. Quiet mind

While in meditation, your mind becomes quiet. Stressors, problems throughout the day, and ways to solve these are stopped while in meditation. People will find it difficult to quiet their minds without any form of practice, although multiple attempts are the key.

2. Being in the Now

Meditation does not concern with the past or the future. All forms of meditation are only concerned with staying in the present and experiencing what is currently happening and then letting it go, and repeating the process. This takes practice as we are all attuned to thinking of the past and the future and not so much with what we have currently.

3. Altered State of Consciousness

When those who practice meditation have achieved a level of proficiency in thinking of the present and having a quiet mind, they reach an altered level of consciousness. This altered state of consciousness is akin to a place between the wakeful state and the sleeping state.

Meditation is associated with increased brain activity in regions of the brain that is connected to happiness and positive thoughts and emotions. Regular practice has been shown to provide prolonged positive effects.

Relaxing the mind is an important step in achieving a healthier intuition. With so much of the world around us drowned in noise, we begin to lose sight of the important things around us. We lose the things that had once held a high degree of importance to our daily lives such as intuition. In attempting to relax our minds, the noise that had once drowned us is filtered out and we begin to see again the important things. We begin to live our lives the way that it should be.

CHAPTER 3

POWER OF PRAYER AND ASKING

Martha, a mother of three, was doing the most stressful thing a mother could do, choosing a childcare provider.

She found a less expensive option in their town which gave a live video stream of your child. But she was torn between another option which was more expensive. Even though times were tough for Martha at that moment, her intuition kicked in as she felt something was off with the cheaper option.

It turns out; the cheaper provider had its place catch fire just a couple of weeks after Martha had decided to go with the more expensive option. Fortunately, no one was hurt in the fire. The place was closed and went out of business.

After the event, Martha had this to say, "Always trust your intuition especially, and I can't stress this enough, with your kids."

1. **A prayer in life and why we should do it. A short explanation of why it is important and some examples of people it has helped in history**

James 5:16-18 declares, "The prayer of a righteous man is powerful and effective. Elijah was a man just like us. He prayed earnestly that it would not rain, and it did not rain on the land for three and a half years. Again, he prayed, and the heavens gave rain, and the earth produced its crops."

This represents an illustrative example that God undoubtedly hears our prayers and answers them as well. That's why no-one should underestimate the immense power of it. Prayer is actually our conversation with God.

Why do we pray? Why should we pray?

Some people today have asked similar questions but as all who practice prayer daily know, we pray because we are communicating with God.

If one wants to be a utilitarian in reasoning, we pray because it is a powerful tool that God has given us. Through prayer, we can ask God, through His goodwill, things to help us fulfill our destiny.

Prayer is so powerful that throughout human history, prayer has been the deciding factor. From ancient Rome to the forests of Belgium, stories have told of prayers being answered, of men living to see another day.

There are also many examples of answered prayers in the Bible, and these are the three most prominent historic examples:

The Battle of the Bulge

"Almighty and most merciful Father, we humbly beseech Thee, of Thy great goodness, to restrain these immoderate rains with which we have had to contend. Grant us fair weather for battle. Graciously hearken to us as soldiers who call upon Thee that, armed with Thy power, we may advance from victory to victory, and crush the oppression and wickedness of our enemies and establish Thy justice among men and nations."

Third Army Chaplain Colonel James O'Neill

It was one of the bloodiest battles in World War II and in American History but was also the greatest triumph of the power of prayer.

It was the 16th of December 1944, when a combined effort of the remaining German tank units and troops had surprised and encircled some 12,000 men in the little town of Bastogne, Belgium. The Allies were caught by surprise as it did not believe that the Germans could attack through the Ardennes Forest (the forest beside Bastogne).

The Germans thought that they had the upper hand and would have an easy fight. When requested to surrender, United States Brigadier General Anthony McAuliffe had replied "NUTS!" For seven whole days, the outnumbered 101st Airborne valiantly fought the forces of the Third Reich.

Although the US Forces had so far defended the town to the Germans, they knew that without help from Patton's Third Army, they will have to surrender. Adding to the situation was the bad weather; Patton only had 24 hours of good weather to send reinforcement to the besieged troops in Bastogne.

Knowing how dire the situation was, Patton had requested the chaplain of the Third Army, Colonel James O'Neill to write a prayer. According to Patton, he wanted a prayer that would clear the weather for the Third Army to travel to Bastogne and help the now dwindling US Forces.

O'Neill quickly drafted the prayer and soon the prayer was on wallet-sized cards distributed to every serviceman.

O'Neill's efforts were not in vain as soon after the prayer had worked. The weather had miraculously cleared, and Patton's Third Army was soon roaring towards Bastogne.

For his efforts, O'Neill was awarded the Bronze Star for "writing a prayer."

Dunkirk Evacuation

It was May 1940, World War II was underway and Adolf Hitler's Germany had caught the allies off guard: France and Belgium were burning. Allied troops on the north of France have been surrounded by German troops on all three sides, with the fourth one facing the sea – they were trapped. It was a very dire situation; the Germans were boasting to annihilate the entire British Expeditionary Force in Dunkirk. Prime Minister Winston Churchill was preparing to deliver the news that more than three hundred thousand British soldiers were captured or killed – the entirety of the troops in Dunkirk.

While the situation in Dunkirk was transpiring, King George VI had called for a National Day of Prayer. Knowing the slaughter that could be, the entire British people devoted their time to prayer that day – this was their last hope. While the people rallied for those left in Dunkirk, the military had made plans to evacuate all soldiers no matter the cost. There was only one problem, there were not enough ships to assist the surrounded troops at Dunkirk.

The British military, in a bid to save the troops in Dunkirk, had asked all vessels available to head to Dunkirk, through the rough English Channel and rescue as many as they can – more than 800 vessels, mostly small yachts and fishing boats, answered the call.

As the Allies made a desperate race for time on what looks like a disaster waiting to happen, Hitler ordered his troops to halt their advance. He wanted the Luftwaffe (German Air Force) to take "pot shots" at the surrounded troops, demoralizing them for the end that was to arrive. Three days went by and Nazi troops and tanks stood idle as the Allies frantically rescued what remained of Dunkirk.

For what could be described as a miracle, bad weather had

grounded the Luftwaffe while the Allies evacuated the British troops. Even though bad weather grounded the Luftwaffe, the ships transporting the troops were treading on calm seas further speeding up the evacuation until everyone was off the beaches of Dunkirk.

The massive evacuation has been touted as the "Miracle of Dunkirk" for it was nothing short of a miracle. A lot of things could have gone wrong that fateful day, but it didn't, from the weather enabling the Luftwaffe to Hitler ordering the siege to continue. Historians are still baffled as to why the evacuation at Dunkirk was made possible.

Battle of Milvian Bridge

Prayers being a very powerful instrument haven't been present in just the modern era. Prayer has also been a deciding factor in a lot of historical events prior to the 20th Century. In fact, prayer has been recognized as what helped the first Christian Roman Emperor win his battle.

It was the 28th of October 312 AD, and a fierce battle was being waged by two Roman Emperors against each other who were fighting for the control of the entire Roman Empire. The battle was against Valerius Constantinus and Maxentius. The fighting was done on Milvian Bridge, a crucial point in the Tiber River. Whoever wins will decide the fate of the empire, those who are in it and countless other lives after it.

The evening before the battle, Constantinus had a vision calling, an answer to his previous prayers. In his vision, he was commanded to mark the shields of his soldier with the "heavenly sign", a Latin cross that denoted Christ. Constantinus was quick to follow his vision and when the fighting ended, Constantinus was found the victor.

Constantinus attributed his victory to the Christian God and His Son, Jesus Christ. The victory at Milvian Bridge paved the way for the first Christian Roman Emperor. The religion had continued since then to what is the Roman Catholic Church today.

Most of the people these days do not find prayer as a powerful tool. When someone is told that prayers would answer their troubles no matter how difficult life is, most are quick to dismiss the advice. But as we have read through, throughout history, prayer has had long-standing consequences.

Prayer changed the direction of history and has saved countless lives. It has shaped our history in a lot of ways that are unimaginable. If it can change the course of history, it can help an individual overcome any and all obstacles in life. So, the next time you encounter difficulty or any troubles, all you must do is pray, and it will be answered.

2. **The power of knowing and clear focus in asking. How will a person know what they want if they don't ask?**

Staying focused sounds simple, but it actually isn't, and like intuition, it needs to be practiced.

When the matter in question is too delicate, we usually choose some softer word, sweeten the conversation up, and fluff it maximally, and the focus is gone.

What we should actually do is hit the core of it and ask PRECISELY what we are interested in.

By saying it directly, we actually confirm both to ourselves and our listeners what is it that we want exactly.

If we stray from the focus, we risk losing our own train of thoughts, and the listener's concentration will consequently decrease. That's why hitting the point matters a lot.

So, the next time that you might need prayer, ask yourself what you really want. Accept it in yourself that it is what you really want and speak of it as if the other person is you – already knowing what you are going to say.

Don't waste time. Focus on what you truly want to say and deliver the message across.

1. Different types of prayers

From the religious point of view, types of prayers vary based on the purpose they are meant for. They can be:

Prayers of Faith

Prayers of Faith are primarily used to save someone who is sick as "the Lord will raise them up". These prayers are offered to someone who is undergoing sickness or health issues. We pray for God to heal these individuals. It is called prayers of faith because we believe in the goodness and power of God to heal. See James 5:15/Mark 9:23.

Prayers of Request (Supplication)

As the name implies, these prayers are done when we request to God. If one request something from God, then it should be made clear to Him, it should be requested from Him. God does not want us to carry the burden of anxiety when there are things; we look for instead he wants us to tell him through prayer. See Ephesians 6:18/Philippians 4:6.

Prayers of Worship

There is very little difference between the prayer of worship and prayer of thanksgiving. But one of the discernible differences is that a prayer of worship is more into the thought of who God is while thanksgiving is into what God has done.

The religious leaders in Antioch had prayed the same manner as the prayer of worship in their fasting.

If we look into Acts 13:2-3, it is stated "Set apart for me Barnabas and Saul for the work to which I have called them. Then after fasting and praying, they laid their hands on them and sent them off". See Acts 13:2-3.

Prayers of Agreement (Corporate Prayer)

This type of prayer is named as the prayer of the agreement because it requires two or more people to come together, to come into an agreement.

As stated in Matthew 18:19, "Again I say to you that if two of you agree on earth concerning anything that they ask, it will be done for them by My Father in heaven. For where two or three are gathered together in My name, I am there in the midst of them"

It means that if people come together in prayer, God will hear them and answer them. See Acts 1:1-4/Acts 2:4-2/Matthew 18:19.

Prayers of Thanksgiving

It might not be good to hear, but most of the time we only pray, we only talk to God when we ask him something for ourselves. Prayer is a form of communication with God and communication is not the same as a one-way conversation.

We must learn to thank God as well. There are many things to be thankful to our Lord; there is no shortage of blessings. We should include a prayer of thanks. See Philippians 4:6.

Prayers of Imprecation

Prayers of Imprecation can mostly be found in the book of

Psalm. The Psalmists use this to call upon God's judgment on the wicked defending the righteous.

Aside from calling upon God's judgment, the prayer also tells of God's holiness and the infallibility of His judgment. Prayers of Imprecation could also be used to ask God for a blessing unto our enemies instead of cursing them as Jesus had once taught. See Matthew 5:44-48.

Prayers of Intercession

So far, most of the prayers that you've read in this chapter are about YOU communicating to God. But there are instances wherein we might want to pray for somebody else, whether that be our parents, children, partners, or our neighbors.

In cases where we pray for others, it is said that we are interceding, thus we call those prayers as prayers of intercession. See Timothy 2:1/John 17.

Prayers of Consecration

Prayers of Consecration act as a way of dedicating yourself to God, may that be your relationship, work, home, or hobbies. We can dedicate to God anything that requires God's grace.

The act of dedication brings any and all our works into God's kingdom and rule.

Dedicating our works to the Lord makes success and happiness even more special than it already is. See Matthew 26:39.

Whatever it is that you may want to pray with God, make sure that you do it often. Talking to God not only lets Him help us, but it also clears our mind of any anxiety or fear. By praying to God, we leave behind all that is negative knowing that God is beside us.

CHAPTER 4

FORGIVENESS

A teenager named Jenny had the sudden feeling that she was being watched inside her home through her window. She had informed her fiancé previously about the feeling that someone was looking at her.

Later that day, she heard a knock on her back door. She attempted to look through the door's peephole and saw a little boy knocking. She had later found out that the little boy was found missing by his parents for no less than an hour and police were already on their way.

According to Jenny, her neighborhood was in an area with dense trees, hills, and animal activity. If she hadn't been on the lookout for the unknown person, then there could have been a high possibility that the boy would've been injured or lost.

It was more than likely that she wouldn't check her back door when the boy knocked if it weren't for her intuition.

1. What is Zero-Point thinking and how does it apply to forgiveness?

What is Zero-Point Thinking?

It is also known as zero-based thinking (ZBT) and it represents a decision-making process in which we imagine ourselves back at the point before certain decisions were made, and using the current knowledge about their outcome, we make those decisions in a specific way.

The technique was first pioneered by the famous self-development author and motivation public speaker Brian Tracy.

According to Tracy, the difference between people who are at the top and those who are in the middle is that the former strives to get out of their comfort zone. They enjoy taking calculated risks and are not afraid to fall back down.

To some individuals, going out of your comfort zone can be very difficult. The false perception of difficulty and our aversion to change also complicates our desire to take risks. So, instead of jumping head-on, Tracy created the Zero-Based Thinking Method.

By asking yourself if you would've done something differently, it opens you up to the truth, to what you truly want. When the truth becomes obvious to us, taking the risks to achieve becomes much easier to swallow. We are propelled to get out of our comfort zone by the answer that we get from what is basically asking ourselves what we truly want.

The purpose of this process is to avoid repeating mistakes from the past, avoiding risk or failure and encourage actions that have turned out to work well or maximize the chances to succeed.

Such a condition may help us understand certain situations or people much better from a different perspective, and forgive him/her in case some mistakes were made.

Using the same logic, we can expect someone to forgive us when we do something wrong or hurt somebody.

Using ZBT, we can make forgiveness much easier. Without constantly thinking of anger, hatred or plotting revenge against someone our mind gets relaxed. A clear mind can do a lot of magnificent things as we've known in the previous chapters.

If forgiveness truly is difficult, then psychologists suggest following these seven truths in order to facilitate the process:

1. Forgiving does not mean that you are at fault

Some people may find forgiveness as a sign that they were at fault. You can forgive yet still maintain the fact that you had not done any wrong. Forgiving does not invalidate the experience that you had felt including the anger, pain and all the other negative feelings associated with it.

2. Forgiveness isn't forgetting

The old saying "forgive and forget" is entirely incorrect. Giving forgiveness to someone does not mean that you must forget it. It is not a prerequisite to forgiveness either that you must forget. What you have experienced was real and deserves to be remembered.

The more proper thing to do is acceptance. Accept that it had happened and that it does not define you or will it impede you in the future.

3. Forgiveness is for your wellbeing

It is widely accepted in the field of medicine that keeping anger inside you has a whole list of negative effects on your health and wellbeing. Also, you may be quick to notice that it would not be beneficial, specifically in receiving support from the people around you, if you continue to radiate an aura of anger, resentment, and bitterness.

Forgiving is something that you do for yourself and not for others. You are not going to forgive because it would benefit the other person, but to release yourself from the shackles of hate.

4. Having the other person apologize or accept your forgiveness is not a prerequisite

You do not need anything from the person who had wronged you. It does not matter if they apologize nor would it matter if they accept the forgiveness.

Unfortunately, a lot of people do not appreciate it, nor do they understand forgiveness. A lot will not even acknowledge what they did was wrong. It is a tough cookie to swallow and you will encounter people of varying degrees of awfulness.

But, then again, forgiveness is for you and not for others.

5. The secret to forgiveness is to let go.

Anger is the main reason why a lot of people find it hard to forgive. Having been wrong, the common instinct is to get back at your enemy and we sometimes foster these negative feelings to the detriment of our selves.

Let go of the anger and move forward. Take note that letting go of anger does not mean forgetting what had happened. Letting go of anger gives you the ability to forgive and find better places. Places where you ought to be.

6. Forgiving is a sign of weakness.

If one thing is for sure, that is forgiveness is not a sign of weakness. Forgiveness does not denote anything. It doesn't mean that you are a foolish, weak, or naïve.

Forgiving simply means that you have fully understood that there are better things for you, and you have seen those things. You are moving forward because you want to be in a better situation.

7. Forgiveness is a process.

Finally, forgiveness is not a word, phrase, or sentence you utter. Forgiveness is a journey and not an answer. You may never fully forgive somebody but knowing that you have chosen the path to forgive is a whole magnitude better than having yourself filled with anger.

CHAPTER 5

ATTITUDE

Shiela was 29 weeks into her pregnancy. Everything was fine according to her doctor and that she should expect a good delivery. But she felt that something wasn't right.

According to her, at the time, her baby just wasn't "moving more". Shiela was in a state of distress as she didn't know what to do and worse – that something wrong was about to happen. Shiela felt the need to check in with her doctor. When her baby was checked, she found out that the baby was beyond the normal heart rate and was going through a heart failure if it continued to beat so fast.

Because of the circumstance, her baby was delivered early with a slim chance of surviving.

Her baby boy is now a grown-up and Shiela can't forget how her intuition had saved her son's life at that moment.

1. The battle within to tune the mind to a negative or positive thought

Divide and Conquer is the usual strategy that is generally employed in war. They create infighting within the enemy's ranks and when the enemy is weakened, they attack.

The same can be said with our selves. When we are confused about what we want to happen when we are unsure, infighting within our very self happens. When this happens, we are weakened, and we are unable to defend ourselves from the challenges of the world.

Some people will see the glass as half-full while the others will see it as half-empty, and that's exactly what defines us the best.

No one says life is all about cupcakes and rainbows but looking at things from some brighter perspective is a huge motivational factor for us to keep moving no matter what.

Similar to the abovementioned skills and techniques, it has to be practiced every day, by starting with some simple "exercises", and gradually moving to more complex situations.

2. **How the human mind is structured for survival and always starts with a negative thought, but if we only focus on the positive things, in the long run, positive things can happen.**

Talk of clear intention and positive thought with daily gratitude.

The strong instinct for survival is the "main guilty" we always have negative thoughts as the starting point.

But the main trick is in creating the right perspective and looking at the situation a bit further, by projecting it into the future.

If something positive is expected as the final outcome, our entire journey should be paved with positive thoughts as well.

Similar to value the importance of the right focus, the right, and clear intentions are the key ingredients to guide us to the ultimate goal.

Clear intentions should be accompanied by gratitude because that way we will continuously encourage ourselves that we are doing the right thing.

Think of it as a string of small victories, which will result in the final and the most magnificent goal - mission accomplished.

CHAPTER 6

UNIVERSAL FLOW OF GUIDANCE

Melissa was asked by her parents to stay at their house while they were out on a vacation. Her dad had recently renovated the house and cleaned out the attic.

It was late in the evening and Melissa was in the guest room watching some movies when she felt a strange feeling asking her to hide in the attic. Melissa couldn't ignore the feeling as it was growing louder and louder. Melissa soon vacated the guest room and went up the attic and went through reading a photo album.

She later heard steps inside the house with things sounding as if the place was being ransacked. Melissa decided to hide inside the attic while waiting for the sound to die down.

When she felt that it was safe, she went down to find the whole place was ransacked – the house was robbed. She immediately called 911 and informed her parents about the situation.

If it weren't for her listening to her intuition, Melissa could have been in a far worse situation.

1. Paths of the subconscious mind

Around 90% of our mind is actually our subconsciousness and it gathers the following parts of our personality; values, habits, long-term memory, beliefs, emotions, imagination, protective reactions, and intuition.

But what is the subconscious mind?

The subconscious mind is a depository of everything that we are and everything that makes us wonderful. The subconscious could contain a lot of things and still has room for it. It has your experiences, memories, beliefs and all that you have gone through.

The subconscious mind also performs the task of creating "automated processes" that takes the brunt of your daily routine. Your day isn't a slow tread because most of the things you do are done automatically by your subconscious sparing your much-needed attention and saving it from when you would truly need it.

Take for example having your first smartphone, in the beginning, you learn how to use your phone and the thousands of bells and whistles common with today's smartphones. Using the phone takes time; it has all your attention. You invest your attention to it because you want to learn as much as you can.

Now compare that to how you are using your phone today. The memory of using the phone has been integrated already into your subconscious. You swipe at your phone, open the apps, sometimes without batting an eye and all in seconds. You can now do things simultaneously without thinking of using your smartphone.

Your subconscious is doing everything for you, day and night for the entirety of your life.

In the subconscious is where our intuition resides. Intuition being an "automated process" itself the more we empower our subconscious the more powerful our intuition becomes.

2. Your journey and no one else's. Stick to your thoughts and don't conform

This certainly doesn't mean you should be stubborn and

disobedient, but focus on your own vision and mission, and be determined to reach it.

That's why you need to plan it carefully and be fully aware of what are the possible ups and downs during the journey.

Our subconscious, therefore our intuition, works best if we structure it around which one we are. By building and strengthening our subconscious using our true self as templates, we increase the accuracy of our intuition.

Copying it from somebody else may affect how our intuition functions. We are all different and our intuition, for it to work, must be tailored fit for everyone.

Try your best to be prepared, ask for advice if you have some doubts, but never ever conform.

3. Unconscious mind

The idea of the unconscious mind came from a well-known psychologist, Simon Freud. Freud envisioned the entire mind as an iceberg. The parts above the water represent our conscious mind while all parts below it are said to be our unconscious mind.

Looking at an iceberg, the portion that is above water is only a small percentage of the entire iceberg. Most of the iceberg is hidden away beneath the waves. Freud posits that the unconscious mind is magnitudes larger than our consciousness.

The unconscious mind (or the unconscious) refers to the processes in the mind which occur automatically. These processes are not available to introspection and include several crucial aspects such as thought processes, memories, interests, and motivations.

According to Freud's Psychoanalytic Theory, the unconscious mind is where we store our thoughts, memories, urges, and feelings that are beyond our conscious mind.

As far as empirical evidence suggests, this aspect of our mind includes repressed feelings, automatic skills, subliminal perceptions, and automatic reactions. In addition to this, it most certainly encompasses complexes, hidden phobias, and desires.

Without us knowing much, our unconscious mind continues to influence us throughout the day, both in our experiences and our behavior.

Freud thought that a lot of our basic urges and the building blocks of our intuition are stored in our unconsciousness. Many of what is stored in our unconsciousness are repressed according to Freud as it is deemed threatening.

Freud reasons that the cause of this repression is due to our conscious mind (our state when we are awake) seeing the contents of our unconscious as irrational or unacceptable. Though, "defense mechanisms" will prevent these contents from spilling into our conscious self.

How does this relate to our intuition?

As mentioned in our early chapters, our culture emphasizes rational thinking and shuns intuition. Since we deem social norms as the "law of the land", we attempt to conform to these norms. We attempt to suppress what is in our unconscious fearing that the society we have grown upon may throw us away the moment that we open the abilities of our unconscious.

1. Consciously subconscious

This is one of the most recent trends in which people started to refer to unconsciousness as a useful tool, a sort of wisdom that they should cooperate with instead of ignoring it.

This trend has been a complete opposite of what our society has been told to emphasize. Now, more and more people have concluded that our unconscious mind is a valuable tool in living our lives to the fullest.

Steps have been taken to mitigate the damage that has been done by centuries of faulty teaching, centuries of moving away from our capabilities as individuals.

Much of the information on the use of our unconscious has been lost. Although, we can still uncover its secrets and salvage what we can.

This is possible provided that you learn what the unconscious mind is and how it works.

It is like a small child, and communicates through symbols and emotions, learns quickly…and after accepting this as its integral characteristic, you will know how to apply it.

2. Consciously superconscious

"Individuality itself seemed to dissolve and fade away into boundless being", - Alfred, Lord of Tennyson when asked what Superconsciousness is.

This state is also known as the higher self, and one can reach it through meditation. It's the state where we are completely liberated from any bondage, a stage above subconscious and conscious.

To put it simply, Superconsciousness is awareness to its fullest. It is the maximum use of our intuition by filtering out the noise that is brought by reason and emotions.

This is the stage where healing and true intuition are reached and can be applied correctly throughout everyday life.

The Superconsciousness lies above the subconscious mind and the conscious mind. Unlike the subconscious that invokes dreams, sleep, and the relaxation of energy in the mind and body, Superconsciousness raises the soul into a highly peaceful and energetic state.

The psychologist, Frederic Myers, once said on precociousness as "the treasure-house, the region that alone can explain the great, unselfish, heroic deeds of men," describing the power that lies in the fathoms of our Superconsciousness. At the level of Superconsciousness, true intuition is made available to us. We realize that it is the true form of being and not an altered state like the subconscious or conscious. We are freed from our limitations and or bondage that we encounter daily with this state of mind.

CHAPTER 7

HEARING AND KNOWING WITH FAITH

It was the middle of the night when George had heard his smoke alarm blaring. George went into the kitchen to find that it was not on fire. He thought that it could have been a false positive or the alarm was faulty.

George reset the alarm and went to sleep only to be awakened by it blaring off again. George looked at the kitchen only to find it okay, but he felt that something wasn't right. So, instead of going back to sleep he called the fire department to have the place checked.

The town where George lived is a small town. But their fire department was very capable in a host of situations. And this circumstance is so odd; George wanted someone who could check everything before he turns in for the night.

Immediately, the fire department sent in multiple fire engines. It turns out that it wasn't fire that was tripping the alarms but carbon monoxide.

According to the fire department, if George had gone back to sleep, he might not have woken up. Carbon monoxide is odorless and colorless and so it would have been possible that he and his family asphyxiated while sleeping.

1. Environment changes – problems and how to change

Accepting change is never easy but needs to be done. We

change constantly and the world around us as well, so embracing it and accepting the whole process as normal and inevitable will simplify our lives.

As humans, we are all but averse to the idea of change. Change is risky albeit it is the only constant thing in the world. Avoiding change, following our nature, only sets us up for failure. We are running away from something that is inevitable. No matter what one does, the change will happen.

All we can do is prepare for what is about to happen to ensure victory. Below are some sources of conflict that you can expect while traversing through the changes in your life.

a. Yourself

It might sound impossible, but you will be your greatest friend and enemy during the change in your life. Humans are risk-averse; we want as little change as possible, minimizing the risks. If your intuition is not up to the task, you will see yourself fighting over the important decisions.

This infighting from within will stagnate you and may cause more harm than the change itself.

b. Family

Your family members have the same inkling as you. But know that they are family. Have them understand the journey ahead and let them know that the family will always be one, regardless of the changes to come. Ease their minds and unify each other towards a common goal. Again, we must avoid in-fighting.

c. People

Your peers, your friends, and everyone else have a say as well with changes. With every culture, there will be a set boundary for change. You will be pressured to conform.

In order to lessen the pressures of conformity, ensure that your goal is clear. A mind that has its target insight will never waiver.

Now, that you have a general knowledge of where obstacles may present themselves, let us look at a couple of ways that we can improve our resiliency with change:

d. Evaluate How Much You Can Control

When change does arrive, we may lose control of the situation. Our focus may be splintered into lots of places either with the events or with the people (whom we have no control over their actions or attitudes) surrounding us.

Do not waste resources on focusing on the things which you have no control over, this includes people and events. Filter out the things that you cannot control and exert all your attention towards the things that you can control.

If you feel powerless over the situation, give power to yourself by looking for the things that you could control.

e. See the Pattern Your Mind Makes

The pressures of change can force your mind to make shortcuts that are not beneficial. Your view of things might get clouded, narrow down to a couple of options, or have you in a grip of fear.

Find the time to examine your thought process, clear up your mind and assess the situation. Again, knowing what you can control is key. If this is difficult for you, you may want to attempt mind relaxation techniques like meditation, mindfulness, and deep breathing. Once your mind is relaxing you may see the opportunities that would allow you to take hold of the situation.

You may cultivate positive thinking during this time by taking note of the previous challenges you might have encountered. Remind yourself of your previous victories.

Focus on your strengths and double down your efforts.

f. Have a Habit of Self-Care After a Loss?

Changes can be good in nature and they may also be bad. There would be cases where change entails a loss; it may be in the form of a change in employment, death, the end of a relationship, or graduation.

When such a transition happens, do not deny it. Accept what is transpiring now. Learn from the situation.

You may seek support from your family, friends, counselor, religious leader, or a mental health professional if required. Take note that this moment in your life requires all the support that you can muster.

g. Live in the Moment

During periods of change, you may be swayed into locking yourself in the past or daydream into the future. When you get pulled, either in the past or the present, your attention may miss the important things.

Remember that during such changes, you need to ensure to live in the moment so that you can observe what is happening. Walk back and make sure that you are living in the moment. If you find yourself swayed to the future or the past, pull yourself back.

Pay attention to how your mind and body react to stress. Give time for your body to relax every day. Do meditation or breathing exercises.

h. Be Clear About Your Priorities

"Set your mind on a definite goal and observe how quickly the world stands aside to let you pass." - Napoleon Hill.

We cannot stress this enough but a mind that has a clear set goal can lead to countless victories. Such a mind becomes resilient to the stress and fear that changes in our lives entail.

Ask yourself what do you really want?

If that question is too broad for you to make a start, then use the Zero Point Technique as mentioned in the previous chapter. Evaluate your past decisions and ask yourself what you may have done differently.

When you have followed all five of our useful tips, do not forget that if you are still having difficulty you can ask for help, whether it is with your family, friends, or with God – pray.

We are all strong and we can withstand a lot of things that can be thrown at us. But at the end of the day, we are humans and humans have flaws. Do not forget that there will be certain times when we can't, but we can ask for help

1. Attention to the body

Our body is our shell where the mind is accommodated; it's a medium between our mind and the outside world.

It is said that there is a difference between the mind and the brain. Some would argue that they are the same and may vary only depending on the context.

But philosophers of the 20th century beg to differ. They said that the brain is part of the body; a physical construct with billions of cells all firing bolts of electricity in unison to fulfill a role encoded by a strand of DNA.

While the mind is the amalgamation of whom we are, our identities, our true self.

But the mind is encased in the brain, and one without the other is useless. A brain without a soul is all but a lumbering heap of flesh, nothing more. It is a flesh that is cursed to walk the Earth aimlessly. The mind cannot show its magnificence without a physical medium.

And so, throughout this book, we have seen what the mind can do and how we can harness this. We have put great emphasis on the power of the mind and its many wonders.

In our bid to empower our minds, to set it free, let us not forget the importance of our body. If we invest in the wellbeing of our minds yet fail to do the same for our bodies, our efforts would be put in vain.

That's why we need to take good care of it, primarily our health, all types of it (mental, spiritual, and physical).

2. The patient is faith in knowing tomorrow is on the way.

Patience plays an important role in the creation of a mature personality, and by applying it daily, with versatile people, characters and situations, we build and upgrade ourselves.

Our fast-paced life has removed from our patience. Learn to be patient as not all things in life appear in a snap.

The most important things in life and the most fulfilling are the things that take time, things that we have poured effort into.

Faith also matters as it provides the necessary dose of motivation and support to keep us focused on the final goal.

CHAPTER 8

SELF-GUIDANCE AND MEANING OF THE RELIGION OF SIN AND BINDING

1. **Examples of different religious beliefs and being bound to society because of pleasure, but the intuition of the inner voice dies, and the mind takes the path of least resistance.**

Hinduism, Buddhism, Islam, and Christianity are just some of the world's most widely spread religious beliefs (you can add more if you think it's necessary) and all of them come with a certain set of rules.

They play significant roles in shaping our personalities as well as the society we live in, as well as our own character on the top of it all.

Whatever religion we are into, we can be sure that they play a significant role in shaping the cultures that accept them. Social norms are set which can be so powerful that no one dares to have a change of heart.

Sometimes we surrender, to say so, and lose ourselves and inner voice because we wanted to go with the flow and allow being led by society, religion.

Slowly, society makes conformity the utmost priority.

The pressure to conform overrides our mental facilities and we begin to take the path of least resistance. We begin to take the path that would lead us to less and fewer capabilities as our intuition becomes bogged down by the noise.

Since intuition plays a crucial role in the most important part of our life, it wouldn't be farfetched to think that mistakes will be made. Overall, a conformist society will stagnate. This scenario is what we are trying to avoid by ensuring freedoms in both mind and body. We are ensuring that we make use of our capabilities to its fullest extent.

If we put ourselves in the center of it all and have ourselves as the starting point, the inner voice will be heard and will lead us.

CONCLUSION

STAYING TRUE TO YOURSELF

Now that you have a clearer picture of how your mind works, you will have a much better approach to every person you encounter and every situation you find yourself in.

As we went through the chapters listed in this book, you saw the stories of people who used intuition for the better. You have seen in somebody else's eyes how important it is to see beyond rationality, that in a pinch, we might need something quicker.

We have read through the current state of things, how our intuition is being hampered by the way we are currently living. We have read how our culture has emphasized rationality while neglecting the benefits that intuition has to offer.

You have seen the ways in how we can recover our intuition from stagnation. We also read the techniques of meditation and how it can be a tremendous help.

We have read of the many stories of prayers being answered - miracles being recorded through history.

We saw the root of true intuition and the underlying mechanisms that support it.

There are many more things that we can explore. This book is but a small window towards the beautiful gifts that life has to offer, many of which have been lost to time.

Keep in mind that continuous exercise, strong will, and faith in yourself are the ones to help you polish your intuition and learn how it works and how to take advantage of it.

Meditation has also greatly helped in my process of losing weight and coping with life in general. On the next page, there is a bonus happiness challenge to get you started.